A Well-Trodden Path

Tameka Bowman

BookLeaf Publishing

A Well-Trodden Path © 2022

Tameka Bowman

Presentation by *BookLeaf Publishing*

Web: www.bookleafpub.com

E-mail: info@bookleafpub.com

ISBN: 978-93-5744-988-5

First edition 2022

DEDICATION

To the members, moderators and professional supporting members of the Young People's Anxiety Depression and Loneliness Social Support Group: you have all supported me just by being yourselves way more than you know and I'll always be grateful for you. I couldn't have asked for a better group of friends to battle through my mental health journey with, thank you for believing in me, our group and each other.

We're stronger together and know it's okay not to be okay! Let's keep growing.

ACKNOWLEDGEMENT

My beautiful mother, Michelle, for her timeless positive energy and caring nature. I couldn't have become the woman I am today without you and, though words will never find the way to describe my appreciation, I'll still try. I love you.

My (soon to be!) husband Jerome, you scooped me out of the darkness and cradled me close, I would be nothing without your warmth and patience and nowhere without your love. Keep being a good guy… I love you.

And to my good friends along the way who pulled me out of dark places and used such beautiful, comforting words to remind me that life can still be beautiful; Abi, Gosia, Gail and Jo I have to thank in particular. I have so much love for you all.

PREFACE

9 year old me would be so proud of where I am today.

(That's a big thing for me to say)

As a child, I created a tutor group for children who were getting bullied in school because they weren't as good in maths and english. I attempted to write an autobiography when I was 10 and was proudly nicknamed the 'Advice Guru' aged 11. My teenage years were full of every sport I had access to as well as performing in front of thousands and volunteering to support vulnerable adults. All of those things sound like the perfect setup into adulthood, or at least I thought so.

I couldn't have been more wrong.

Losing myself was the worst pain I ever had to endure. All of my social confidence, ambition, cognitive and physical abilities crumpled up and seemingly unable to bounce back like a thin, weary piece of paper.

I chose to write about mental health poems as a part of my journey. Initially, I didn't talk about my issues at all and this caused them to bubble up inside until I finally exploded. Thankfully, I had the support around me that I needed and now know how beneficial it is to be vocal with those around you who care.

I created the Young People's Anxiety Depression and Loneliness Social Support Group in January of 2020 and have had the privilege of creating a safe space to support hundreds of vulnerable people around the world throughout lockdown and beyond. Through pain came hope as we saw the spike of new members during the first UK lockdown yet also gained confidence through zoom calls and friendships through group chats.

It was difficult at times to complete this collection as it is so close to my heart and extremely personal. Finding the words to explain my suffering was also difficult; ; I lost count of how many times I googled "synonym for…" or, "rhyme with..." but I'm so thankful to have this opportunity and for my voice to be heard through poetry.

Taking on this 21-day challenge to publish a poetry book when I haven't written poetry in almost 10 years was an instant reminder of my spontaneous past-self and gave me extra encouragement to remind others too that there is still hope. My biggest aim with this collection is to reach out to those who feel alone or feel like giving up, I want to help spread the word that those beautiful people are not alone.

If you're reading this, you're doing great.

Strength of mind

My depression will always be stronger.
there's no way I can force myself to believe that
there is so much to live for and so much I have
yet to achieve
because, realistically,
everything sucks.
even if
I find joy in a sunrise or hope in my heart
happiness and gratitude won't last.
I'm now less likely to believe that
there is a way out;
with each dark day thrown at me, I see clearer
how trapped I am right now
it just hurts a lot to know
I'm a failure,
I won't let myself believe that
I am stronger than my depression.

Now read it backwards!

Do you feel the rain?

Do you feel the rain? Because I can’t feel a
thing.
It’s been a long time since I last flinched whilst
wet spots scatter, splatter
pit-and-patter on my skin.
The chill that allows many goosebumps to
follow
and the hollow, turbulent emotions from within.

I used to hate the rain, now I just wonder what
it’s like
The inside view of what could be seems more
comforting, less demanding
Yet less upstanding, misunderstanding
Especially to my friends who will ask how I’ve
been and all I can say is
“I can’t feel a thing”

I trace raindrops with light touch, hoping one
day it will smudge.

Self calm

Naked, tired, bruised.
Old scars heal as new art appears
Dripping halts silence.

Fan’s apology

Now the Champions League, then the European
Cup,
Players standing in a line anticipating their
close-up.
I wish I felt that same old thrill that we all felt as
kids,
All I feel watching the screen is the strain behind
my eyelids.
I love my team, I love the game, red runs
through my blood,
Yet trying to find love for myself just seems to
be no good.

“Red army, red army,
Red army, red army!”

It sends shivers down my spine, we’re so close
To the goal line
I cry with happiness
but then I remember happiness doesn’t last
It’ll pass. It’ll pass.

“It's a good job Luke Shaw was switched on,
He did well defending in that two v one”

Watching the game with hollow holes glossed
over by my thoughts
Thoughts overgrown with moss…
Watch that cross!!
Then the pain my thought has brought

It's not just mental, not in my head
It's beating through my chest
thudding; manic and depressed
Sweat drops form upon my neck
I'm stressed
not from the game but this game I play daily
verses myself
Look in the mirror my reflection looks scaly
meds on the shelf
One day im strong enough, the next I'm just not
Its okay not to be okay until the pill pops..
relieve yourself

deep breaths

We've crawled back up from 2-0 now, Ronaldo
got our third
My celebration loud, proud n manc with speech
slurred
Ref calls four final minutes, we're chanting with
the crowd
United Till I Die, we will stick to what we
vowed

The whistle blows, the win is ours
What a time to be alive…
A huge smile spreads across my face
I wish I felt that all the time.

- This page is just for you -

I want you, the reader, to use this space in any way you feel will be positive for yourself. Get creative!

Onto the stage (My Royally Varied Performance)

Onto the stage steps deep depression concealed by jubilation, for the act may have only just started yet my acting had begun.

Days before the day and my mind is slipping further away from hope; my first rehearsal forgotten and thrown away with a lie.

The second was my first and it was apparent that I was able to fit in… yet my heart refused to open to make that space.

Onto the stage steps deep depression concealed by jubilation, for the act may have only just started yet my acting had begun.

I told the kind bearded man when I looked into his eyes that I am depressed and there is nothing that can help my mood today.

He didn't believe me.
Nobody believed me.

"When you come off that stage you'll be
beaming with pride"
"I've done this before, I know how I'll feel
inside"

Onto the stage steps deep depression concealed by jubilation, for the act may have only just started yet my acting had begun.

Curtains closed but not for long and tears pushed down again, replaced with air from my pursed lips. Standing, waiting; sad.

As if ignited by flint itself the fire in my eyes shone brighter than Venus as I was always instructed that "the show must go on" and so it did.

A barren body; a soulless skeleton shining with the poise and promise of performers: "the show must go on"

Onto the stage steps deep depression concealed by jubilation, for the act may have only just started yet my acting had begun.

Hold that smile. Shoulders back. Eye contact with the audience. SMILE. Raise that chin. Purposeful stepping only: click. smile. step. click. s m i l e.

Big faces! More from the back. Feel the lyrics. More teeth! No movement. Silence. First bow. Second bow. Clap. Silence.

IF YOU CAN SEE THE AUDIENCE THE AUDIENCE CAN SEE YOU.

Still. It's strange; I sense everyone's euphoria but my own. Feet rooted. Fade to black. Smile. Arms down. Standing still, waiting; sad.

Finally, Allowed to be depressed again, as if Eeyore himself awakened from a nap; switched off and unaware of the pain for mere minutes then right back into that lonely, dark pit of pity.

Onto the stage stepped deep depression concealed by jubilation, for the act had already started yet my acting had begun.

Clinking glasses trigger my senses, probing leading questions in my head:

“Why aren't I happy?” is the prominent one taking over all thoughts and encouraging tears to daringly drip in such a crowded room.

I have everything. I’m so lucky. Why can’t I appreciate life? I don't deserve anything. What’s the point? I hate myself so much.

And then the train ride to turn things around, watch out depression: I’m Latvia bound.

Onto the stage stepped deep depression concealed by jubilation, for the act had already started yet my acting had begun.

Unseen

The world can’t see me
Screaming, crying, begging: please!
Leave me be unseen.

Will.I.Am

Today I heard the confidence of a man who will
prevail,
"The F in failure stands for flight, it does not
mean you'll fail.
It stands for fearless, flying high…" and then he
stopped to turn:
"Never forget that failure is an opportunity to
learn"

Those words stuck with me through my day and
guided me along
It gently brushed my brain, just as lyrics from a
song.
The idea of changing my mindset seemed an
impossible feat
Till' I came across a crossroad and those bad
thoughts took a seat

"L is a learn, not a loss!" I'll take this to my
grave,
but I know in darker moments my thoughts
likely won't behave.
I'll take the L if it means a lesson, I'm open to
try this way
and if it does go wrong, it's okay not to be okay.

- This page is just for you -

I want you, the reader, to use this space in any way you feel will be positive for yourself. Get creative!

Let go

Let go of your worries, just for today,
Then say the same thing tomorrow.
Find joy in your hum, for no good will come,
From grieving yesterday's sorrow.

Out of sight, out of mind

Suddenly, silence.

Curled on the floor, hours pass,
decision cast
Separated from the mass

Don’t let them see you.

Prickling goosebumps like shards of glass
lay on harsh grass
Waiting for death to pass,

Please pass by.

Please pass fast
Don't let this torment last
This daily torture I can’t surpass

Just, let me die.

I see myself just lying there,
Frozen stiff; body bare

Cold air flees, a fresh and frosty witness to
beware but now, it is my friend.

A true friend comes in cloth of black
He hoists a striving skeleton; my committed
corpse, with bend in back
As my heavy heart grows, sunken misery to
emerge
From depths of which would have been
forgotten to the world.

Till death do us part

Oh, how lovers quarrel amidst fiery fueled feuds;
the passion of fighting words, the hatred to be in love.
The pull of pushing those closest away and the emptiness that follows.

The pain that follows.
The torment.
Burden.

How lowly and wholly one's regrets breaststroke through breath,
Through tears and upset, forever in debt.

The dream

I never had a dream because I couldn't fall asleep,
Too busy racing and tracing back to the day 'this' began just to get a peek of what it truly was
That ruined me
Back to the precise moment
I was damaged beyond repair
Beyond self-care
Prolonged despair
Blankly staring at open walls of white for who knows how long
Earphones tucked tightly to ensure my suffocation, or lack of… this time.
Counting sheep; "be the herd"
Counting beats and repeating words it doesn't help my brain to stop engaging in conversations with itself
Nothing helped.
Through the years came experience, came knowledge and hope
Yet realistically I knew this was a lifetime deal.
A no-go, dead-end, decaying and decadently dangerous deal with Queen insomnia herself.

And when footsteps approach, though I'm already still, my tiny mind screams "BATTLESTATIONS" as I relax my facial muscles and flop my hand recreating realism for my mum's weary eyes.

But I was still way too busy in my mind.
And I stayed way too busy in my mind.

Unloved

Memories of love,
Why did this happen to me?
Life can change so fast.

- The next two pages are challenges -

Choose one challenge to complete on each blank page.

Your challenge choices:
-12 days, 12 lines (Try to write a line of poetry each day for 12 days)
-Snapshot (Write a poem about the first thing you see in front of you)
-Specialist (Choose a specific type of poem to create e.g. limerick/haiku and create a poem about your own experience around mental health)

- Extra page for your challenges -

Choose one challenge to complete on each blank page.

(Try to choose a different challenge than your first)

At night, I am winter

In the morning, I am Autumn, brown
Leaves lightly lowering, sharing, fair
Skin frosts faster in the wind, cold
Looks from strangers feed my anxiety.
At night, I am winter, bitter
Feelings build fast, sweater weather, harsh
Words cut as easy as the end scene.

I once knew a girl

I once knew a girl who was me;
As bold and active as could be!
Then depression came knocking
And her fibro was blocking
the path to unquestionable glee.

I once knew a girl, she was I
Her passion for people - divine
But passion's a priority;
She became the minority
Now there's pain from her toes to her spine.

I once knew a girl, she felt down
'It' seemed to fit her pronoun
Her shoulders overloaded
Until one day she exploded;
a reminder to pick up her crown.

Now, I know a woman.

www.ingramcontent.com/pod-product-compliance
Lightning Source LLC
Chambersburg PA
CBHW051751130826
49812CB00033B/1102
* 9 7 8 9 3 5 7 4 4 9 8 8 5 *